D1530354

The Pawn Queen

Learn the Basics of Chess

Cheryl Hindman

Forward

When I was five years old, my father introduced me to the game of chess. He often played with his brother, my Uncle John, to pass the time in the 1940s, when they were just kids. My dad taught me on the same chess set they used, which I still have today and which served as the basis for the graphics in this text.

I decided to teach my twin sons how to play when they were about five. At that time, I searched for an age-appropriate book at the library, in stores and online, but could only find books detailing high-level strategies or outlining the historical background of the game.

As a graphic designer and aspiring writer, I decided to create my own text. Upon its completion, I shared it with some friends at the library where I volunteered. They loved it, adding it to their circulation and setting up a meet-the-author and introductory chess lesson for the community.

Since then, I've read my book to and offered the same introductory lesson for numerous classrooms and libraries. I often hear from parents about their child's newfound love of chess and how they play all the time! How wonderful for me to be able to share the knowledge my father gave to me with countless children (and often their parents, too).

Although some children will be ready to learn how to play chess as early as age 4, it seems that second grade (age 7 or 8) is a more ideal time to start. Several movies have been made about the game of chess, including Searching for Bobby Fischer (1993) and The Knights of the South Bronx (2005). There are also numerous books and online articles which indicate the behavioral as well as cognitive benefits of chess playing for the developing brain.

*Chess is a game
of strategy.*

The **objective** is to
dethrone the king
of your **opponent**.
You must place him in
checkmate

so he can no longer move
without being captured.

My goal as queen,
and the goal of
all of the pieces, is to
protect my king,
even if it means being
captured by my opponent
in the process.

White *always* moves first, often with the
pawn, the smallest and least powerful piece
on the board. **Plentiful**, but powerless,
the pawn can only move forward.

On his first move, the pawn may
move forward one or two spaces.
After that, the pawn can only
move ahead one space at a time.

I, however, am the *omnipotent queen.*

I can move any way I please in
any direction I want, to any degree.
I can also capture.

The other pieces fear me, yet protect me.
I am more powerful than the king,
for he can only move one space at a time.

The white knight

makes his move:
UP-RIGHT-RIGHT or DOWN-LEFT-LEFT
or LEFT-UP-UP or LEFT-DOWN-DOWN
or RIGHT-UP-UP or RIGHT-DOWN-DOWN.

Always in the shape of an L. **He is** the only piece that can **hurdle** the others.

Alas, my pawn
captures his knight!

The pawn can only
capture diagonally
or sometimes
en passant.

The white bishop

moves **diagonally.**

Each player has **two bishops.** One moves on **the light squares** and the other moves on **the dark squares.**

Moments later, the ebony pawn
captures the white rook,
reaching the other side of the board.
The pawn **queens,** exchanging
its piece for a *second* ebony queen.
We are now a duo of queens:
"true queen" and "pawn queen."

A white pawn captures
the ebony rook
and **queens** as well. **Touché!**

We take turns. Back and forth.
Each piece trying to
dethrone the king.

It seems my last move threatened their king!

He decides to castle.

The white king moves **two spaces** to his right and the **rook jumps over** him

for protection.

Castling can only be done if:

the king **and** rook have not moved, and the king is **not in check** or **checkmate**.

(The rook moves horizontally or vertically.)

Success! I capture their queen, but
am then captured by my opponent.
Our best chance to defeat their king
lies with our own pawn queen.

I take back the mean things
I said about that little pawn, for
now it is more
powerful than I am.

The pawn queen moves,
again and again.
She is relentless.

Check the king. Move the king.
Again and again!
The pawn queen declares
checkmate! Victory at last!

A lesser piece proved to be more
resourceful than me by having
the power to change.

*At least
in the game of chess,
a pawn can be
just as powerful
as a queen!*

The Players

Pawn

The most plentiful, yet weakest piece in the game of chess. Pawns can only move forward, never backward. The first time a pawn is moved, however, it can move forward one or two squares. A pawn can only capture diagonally or *en passant* (see *Additional Terms*).

Bishop

The bishop moves diagonally through any number of unoccupied squares. It can only move on the color on which it begins the game. Bishops cannot jump over other pieces and can only capture another piece by occupying the square on which that piece sits.

Knight

The move of the knight looks like the letter L. The knight can jump over other pieces (of either color) to its destination square. It then captures the piece that sits on the square on which it lands. The knight does not capture any of the pieces it hurdles in the process.

Rook (or Castle)

The rook moves horizontally or vertically, through any number of unoccupied squares. The rook captures by occupying the square on which the opposing piece sits. The rook can also *castle* with the king (see *Additional Terms*).

Queen

The most powerful piece in the game of chess, the queen sits on its own color at the beginning of the game and is able to move any number of squares vertically, horizontally, or diagonally. It captures by landing on the space on which its targeted piece sits.

King

The king is the most important, yet the weakest piece in the game. The objective of chess is to capture the opponent's king. If a player's king is threatened, it is said to be in *check*. If the player cannot remove the threat of capture on the next move, the king is said to be in *checkmate* and the game is over.

Additional Terms

Castling is a means of protecting the king. When castling, the king moves two squares toward the rook, and the rook moves over the king to the next adjacent square. A king may castle to either the right- or left-side of the board (king-side or queen-side, depending on the king's starting color), as long as neither the king nor rook has moved and the king is not in check.

A king is said to be in *check* if it is exposed to attack or threatened to be captured by its opponent. *Checkmate* occurs when the king's escape from capture is impossible.

To *dethrone* is to remove from a powerful position, such as a throne.

En passant occurs when a player (let's say white) moves a pawn two squares forward from its starting position in order to avoid capture by another pawn (ebony). The opposing pawn (ebony) can still capture the first pawn (white) as if it had only moved one square. En passant must be played immediately after the pawn (white) advances two squares, or the right to capture by the opposing pawn (ebony) "in passing" is lost.

A **_hurdle_** is a movable panel, fence or barrier to be jumped in a race. In the case of chess, the pieces over which the knight jumps serve as the hurdle.

Maneuver means to make a movement, or change in direction, toward an objective. Often used as a military term or exercise, but in the more general sense considered a clever move or action.

An **_objective_** is a goal or desired outcome or action.

To be **_omnipotent_** means to have unlimited power or authority.

An **_opponent_** is a person or thing that offers resistance.

Pawn promotion (a.k.a. to queen) occurs when a pawn successfully reaches the last row on the opponent's side of the board. That pawn may "promote" to a queen, knight, rook, or bishop of the same color. The new piece then replaces the pawn on the board. Promotion is not limited to captured pieces, thereby implying that there may be more of a certain piece (i.e. queen), during game play than there were at the beginning of the game.

Additional Terms (cont'd)

<u>*Plentiful*</u> means to be present in large numbers or to have an ample supply.

<u>*Relentless*</u> means to be steady and persistent, not giving way to pressure, and not reducing intensity, strength or pace.

<u>*Resourceful*</u> means to be able to deal well with difficult or new situations.

<u>*Strategy*</u> is the art of making or employing a series of plans, tricks or maneuvers to achieve a specific goal or result.

<u>*Touché*</u> is a fencing term often used by a person to acknowledge a clever move made by an opponent.

Chess Board Diagram

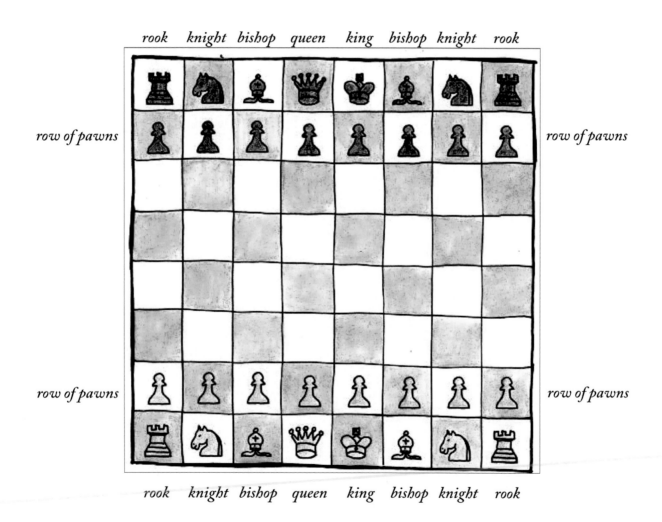

rook knight bishop queen king bishop knight rook

row of pawns   row of pawns

row of pawns   row of pawns

rook knight bishop queen king bishop knight rook

Setting Up the Board

Setting up the board is quite easy for the game of chess.
Just follow these steps and you'll be on your way!

The first step in setting up the board is to make sure that
the square in the lower right-hand corner for each player is white
(or the light-colored square if using a board with different colors).
THINK: "White on right."

Next place the four rooks
(a.k.a. castles) on the four
corners of the board.

THINK: "Castles in the corner."

Place the knights (or horses)
next to their rooks.

THINK: "Horses run from the Castles."

Next place the bishops
(the pieces with a slot in their face)
next to the knights.

THINK: *"Bishops dismount the Horses."*

Place the queen on the square
of its color (white on the light
square and ebony on the dark).

THINK: *"Queen on color."*

Place the king next to the queen.

THINK: "King by his mate."

Finally, place the eight pawns in the row in front of the other pieces.

THINK: "Front row defense."

Moving the Pieces

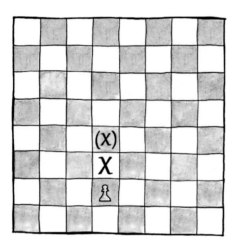

Pawn (Quantity: 8)

The pawn moves forward one square at a time (on its first move, it can move forward either one or two squares). It captures diagonally (and sometimes en passant).

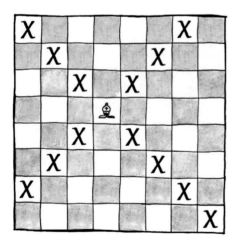

Bishop (Quantity: 2)

The bishop moves and captures diagonally on the color on which it begins the game. It cannot jump over other pieces.

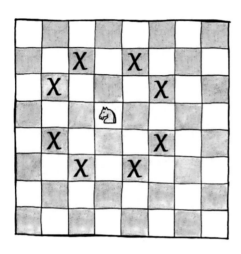

Knight (Quantity: 2)

The knight moves in the shape of an "L" (always 1x2 or 2x1). It is the only piece that can hurdle pieces of either color. It captures the piece on which it lands, and not the pieces over which is passes.

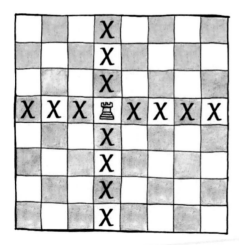

Rook (Quantity: 2)

The rook moves any number of unoccupied squares horizontally or vertically and captures the piece on which it lands. It also participates with the king in castling.

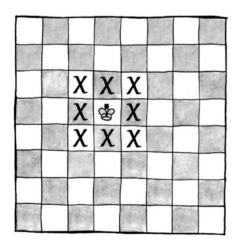

Queen (Quantity: 1)

The queen moves any number of squares diagonally, horizontally and vertically and is the most powerful piece in the game. She captures by occupying the space on which the enemy target sits.

King (Quantity: 1)

The king can only move one square at a time in any direction. The king is in "check" if he is in danger and "checkmate" if he can no longer move. Once checkmate is declared, the game comes to an end.

Bird's eye view of my Dad's chess set, which served as the basis
for the illustrations in this book. I photographed the pieces according
to their playing positions and then used Adobe Photoshop to
modify and render the images as if they were drawings.

28038832R10027

Made in the USA
Middletown, DE
30 December 2015